What the Heart Knows

Chants, Charms & Blessings

by Newbery Honor winner

Joyce Sidman

✻

Illustrations by Caldecott Honor winner

Pamela Zagarenski

HOUGHTON MIFFLIN BOOKS FOR CHILDREN
Houghton Mifflin Harcourt
Boston New York

Houghton Mifflin is an imprint of Houghton Mifflin Harcourt Publishing Company.

www.hmhbooks.com

The text of this book is set in Celestia Antiqua.
The illustrations are mixed media paintings on wood, and computer illustration.

The poem "Riding a Bike at Night" first appeared in the *Christian Science Monitor*.

Library of Congress Cataloging-in-Publication Data

Sidman, Joyce, author.
[Poems. Selections]
What the heart knows: chants, charms, and blessings / written by Joyce Sidman; illustrated by Pamela Zagarenski.
pages cm
ISBN 978-0-544-10616-1
1. Children's poetry, American. I. Zagarenski, Pamela, illustrator. II. Title.
PS3569.I295S63 2013
811'.54—dc23
2012047836

Manufactured in China
SCP 10 9 8 7 6 5 4 3 2 1
4500413781

For Judi, who always listens
—J.S.

For Buttercup, her owl feathers & Bunny
—P.Z.

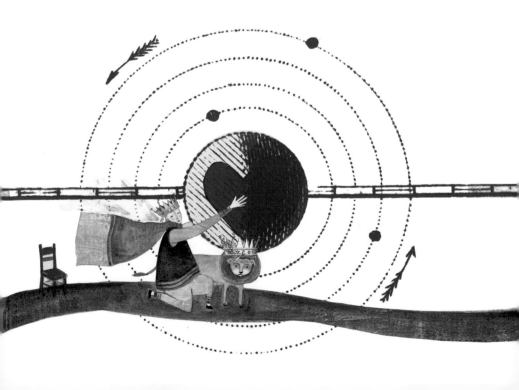

If you say it right, it helps the heart to bear it.

—Mary Oliver

A Note to Readers

WE SPEAK TO SEND MESSAGES TO THE WORLD. We chant for what we want, bless what we like, lament what we've lost. When angry, we curse; when in love, we sing.

We have always done this. Since earliest human history, we have used language to try to influence the world around us: the words *invoke* and *enchant* come from early words for "voice" (*vox*) and "song" (*canto*). We've chanted poems and songs to help win battles, bring rain (or make it stop), bless journeys, and ward off evil. In olden times—when charms were considered highly potent and praise songs averted catastrophe—we filled our lives with poetry from morning till night.

We may no longer believe that words can make crops grow, prevent illness, or keep rivers from flooding. But we still believe in the power of the words themselves. Why else would we pray, sing, or write? Finding phrases to match the emotion inside us still brings an explosive, soaring joy.

I wrote these poems for comfort, for understanding, for hope: to remind myself of things I keep learning and forgetting and learning again. They're about repairing friendship, slowing down time, understanding happiness, facing the worst kind of loss. They are words to speak in the face of loneliness, fear, delight, or confusion.

I hope they work for you. I hope you're inspired to write some of your own—and chant them, in your own voice.

—Joyce Sidman

CONTENTS

Chants & Charms
~ to bolster courage and guard against evil ~

1

Spells & Invocations
~to cause something to happen~

17

Laments & Remembrances
~ to remember, regret, or grieve ~

33

Praise Songs & Blessings
~to celebrate, thank, or express love~

49

Chants & Charms

~ to bolster courage and guard against evil ~

CHANT: A musical recitation of words, used as part of a ritual or assembly, often to lend power or energy.

CHARM: A verse spoken aloud that acts as a talisman or protection.

CHANT TO REPAIR A FRIENDSHIP

(a triolet)

Come, friend, forgive the past;
    I was wrong and I am grieving.
Tell me that this break won't last—
take my hand; forgive the past.
    Anger's brief, but love is vast.
    Take my hand; don't think of leaving.
Come, friend, forgive the past;
    I was wrong and I am grieving.

Come, Happiness

Happiness,
you're not what everyone says:
some flashy friend
who shows up with fireworks,
trailing fame and glory.

You are more like a raindrop,
governed by mysterious principles.
You fall from the sky
and hit—*plop!*—with
a cool kiss of surprise.

Or maybe you're a heartbeat,
always there,
speaking in your low, soft voice,
pumping, warming, strengthening
under the surface of things,
just doing your work.

Happiness, you're like a breeze
sucked in by eager lungs.
You fill and feed us,
and yet somehow, in the exhale,
you are shared.

So come,
come to us, Happiness.
Bathe us with your cool spray.
Fill us with your splendid breath.
Help us do your work.

CHANT AGAINST THE DARK

Don't come close, dark.
Don't brush my face with your sticky hands.
Stay as cool and distant as a train whistle.
Don't single me out,
don't make me answer your questions.
Let me curl here, safe in my circle of light.

Don't come close, dark.
Don't speak to me in your crooked tongue.
I don't want to hear your stories.
I have stories of my own
to tell myself all night.

Don't come close, dark.
Don't breathe on me.
When the lamp clicks off,
don't creak and shift
like some wild-eyed horse
waiting for its rider.

Oh, dark,
don't call my name.

Song of Bravery

This one's not a sure thing.
I'm not bound to win.
I don't think I'll ace it this time.
I won't break a leg,
make my own luck,
or reach the stars.

The sun is not shining on me today.
The force is not strong.
Before the day is out,
I'll taste the grit of dust.

Maybe I didn't do all I could.
Or maybe I did
but there were others who did more.
Maybe I'll never know.

But here I go—
bones clicking quietly together,
blood flowing dutifully
from heart to hands and back again—
here I go, stepping out
through the door
of my own shadow:
into the glare of the arena
to face the lions.

A List of Things That Will Set You Free

Feet.
Wheels.
    Wind.
    Sunshine.
Words.
Music.
    A voice.
    A touch.
Caring.
Not caring.

Saying to yourself:
    I am too old to do this.
    I am too young to do this.
    I am too smart to do this.
    It's not my fault.
    It is my fault, and I will fix it.

    I can do this.

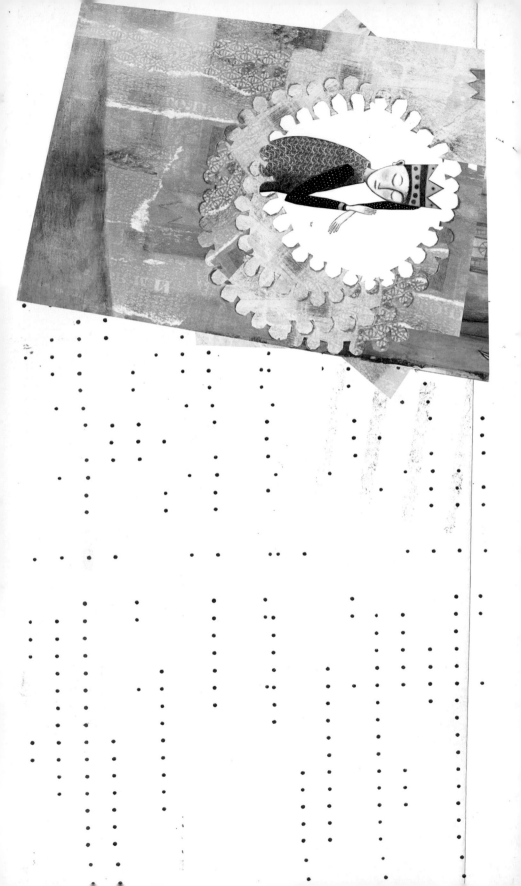

Sleep Charm

This bed is the perfect bed.
Sink into its healing
cloud-softness,
cheek against cool pillow-white.
Forget anything you ever wanted,
hoped, or feared.
One by one, those cares will drop
from you like stones
into deep water.
Slip from your dayskin
and swim, shimmering,
into the dream beyond the dream.

The world will wait for you
through all its dark and absent hours,
and the creatures of the night
will sing your name.

How to Find a Poem

Wake with a dream-filled head.
Stumble out into the morning,
barely aware of how the sun
is laying down strips of silver
after three days' rain,
of how the puddles
are singing with green.
Look up, startled
at the crackle of something large
moving through the underbrush.
Your pulse jumping,
gaze into its beautiful face.
The wary doe's body,
the soft flames of ears.
As it bounds away,
listen to the rhythm
of your own heart's disquiet.
Burn into memory
the white flag of its parting.
Before you return
to house and habit,
cast your eyes into the shadows,
where others stand waiting
on delicate hooves.

SPELLS AND INVOCATIONS

~ to cause something to happen ~

SPELL: Rhythmic words—sometimes accompanied by actions—that are thought to possess the ability to bring about a desired end.

INVOCATION: The act of calling upon or summoning a higher power for help.

Invitation to Lost Things

Come out, come out
from your hidden places,
hair clips, homework, phones.

Come show yourselves,
mittens, earrings, socks.
Come play your part.

Come find your mates,
come cleave together.
There is a place you belong.

For we, careless giants,
don't know your dainty paths,
can't read the maps you follow.

We bow to your littleness,
pencils, glasses, keys.

Without you we are lost
in this big world of ours:

you, who wait so silently
to solve the puzzle of our days.

Time Spells

I. (To Speed Up)

God of Time,
bring forth all galloping things
to thunder through this endless waiting,
split it open like an exploding balloon.
Let the minutes shatter and scurry
with the pounding of feet:
the sound of me running
toward the future.

II. (To Slow Down)

O sweet Time:
stretch like a sleepy dog,
slow and languid and warm
with flickering light.

Let the fire of this moment—
with my friends beside me—
burn
    and burn
        and burn.

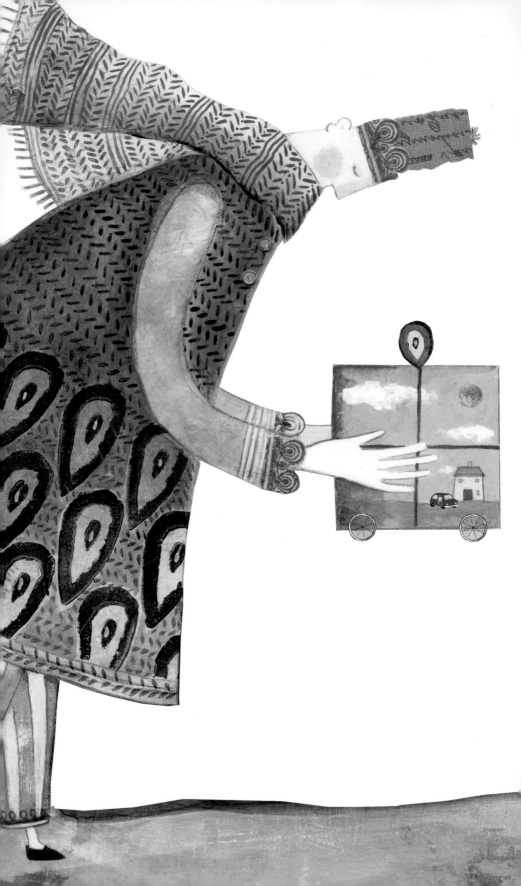

GIFT SPELL

Whatever is inside
that large, flat box:

Let it not be made of wool—snowflake
pattern—one arm slightly longer
than the other, knitted in my formerly
favorite shade of green.
Let it not be square and thick
with stiff covers,
full of wit and wisdom.
Let it not be the hope of a new hobby.
Let it not be anything
to keep me neat, or clean, or safe.

Whatever it is,
let it shrink down
small and hard and cold.
Let it have metal teeth
and a whiff of speed.
Let it slip with a sweet jingle
into my battered jeans
as I run
for the garage.

That box: It looks like something else.
But let it be freedom.

INVOCATION FOR SANDCASTLES

Let all walls, rooms, tables, chairs,
shrink and crumble, soften

to one smooth horizon: wind-snapped sky
and swallowing green water.

Let the beach unroll like a secret smile—
tang of hot skin, rough hug of towel—

and time ease to the wash of waves,
the beat of a gull's cry.

Let the world gleam with the glory of sand:
packed into piles and carved into caverns;

let it cling to all clothing and sandwiches,
linger in wet, salty hair. Let it shift

underfoot, sift into pockets of shells,
gritty and whispering

of days spent in sunlight, building things
that don't need to last.

Invisibility Spell

When taunting eyes chill me,
when laughter stings like sleet,

let my blush blaze hot,
melting each frozen bone.

Let heat pour from my fingers,
turning snow to puddles,

puddles to lakes,
lakes to sultry mist.

Who needs this heavy coat of shame?
Beneath it
I burn with beauty.

It is spring.
I belong to the air.
I step from my body,
invisible.

Song in a Strange Land

I awaken in a village
on a mountain
far from anything
I have ever known.

My eyes are no use—
the dark is that deep—
and my ears
buzz with silence.

No ripple in the black,
no chink in the quiet.
Unmoored,

I could rise, teeter,
tumble down the hillside,
drown in the sea.
Why am I not afraid?

Amazed, my heart
waits for direction.

And there—oh!
A rooster has found the dawn.
Its peal arcs through dark,
waking the circling hills
till the valley rings
like a steel drum.

Oh, yes,
says my heart.
Whatever the day brings,
let it bring.
Whatever the music,
let me sing.

MAGNETIC

NORTH

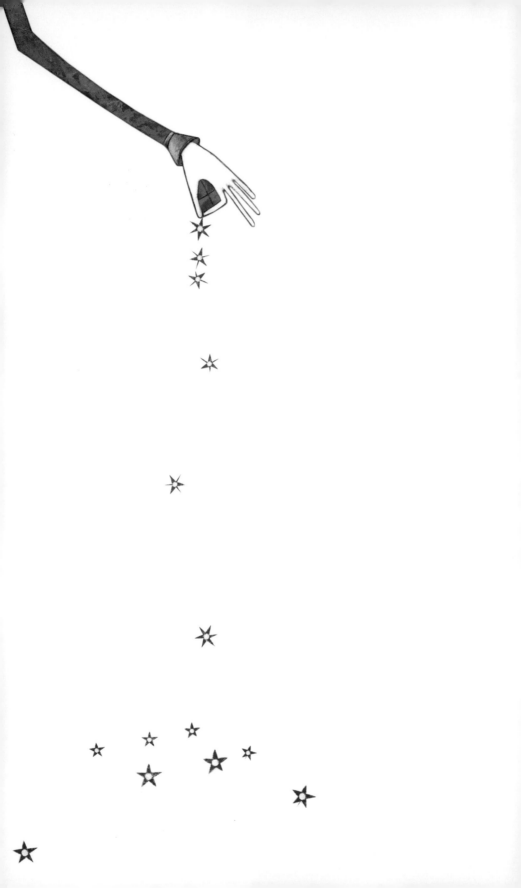

Starting Now

It is time for us to wake:
we who stumble through the day
with our gripes and complaints,
who drift numbly
through thronging halls and streets —

you and I,
who rant about injustice,
who see all that is wrong in this world
but believe we are shackled
and powerless.

It is time to look into
each other's faces,
we who glide along the surface,
time to dive down
and feel the currents
of each other's lives.
Time to speak until the air
holds *all* of our voices.
Time to weave for each other
a garment of brightness.

Open your eyes.
Feel your strength.
Bless the past.
Greet the future.

Join hands.
Right here.
Our moment:
starting now.

LAMENTS & REMEMBRANCES

~ to remember, regret, or grieve ~

LAMENT: A poem or song expressing grief or loss.

REMEMBRANCE: A memory or recollection concerning a particular person, place, or thing.

LAMENT FOR TEDDY

(an ubi sunt)

Where is that softest of bedfellows,
whose battered nose hung askew?
Whose slack head lolled
but whose eyes sang through the dark
to buttress my dreams?
Whose tongue lapped the lint
of many beds?
Whose scent swallowed all nightmares?
Whose balding ears drank in
secrets and wonderings,
passion and venom equally
without a shiver?

Whose fur unfurred,
whose plush unplushed,
whose threads of claws
spindled and popped,
all in service to his queen?

Where is the one
whose mute love followed me
all the days of my life?
The one I boxed up and packed away?
The one I thought I didn't need?
The one I felt
    I had outgrown?

WHERE IS MY BODY?

(an ubi sunt)

Where is my body?
The one I'm used to,
slim and ordinary as a twig?
What happened to the scabby knees,
forgettable front,
hips that were not really
hips at all?

Where is the hair
that shed clips like needles,
its part a soft pathway
through shining woods?
And my face—
where are the bright, fearless eyes
and elastic mouth,
the nose that sat like a gumdrop
on smooth gingerbread skin?

Where is the body
that housed an
Olympic gymnast,
sumo wrestler,
pirate,
dancer;
all waiting, poised
in endless possibility?

When did I grow
awkward, lumpish,
a stranger in my own skin—
each day revealing
some fresh freakishness?

Where is my body—the one I loved,
the one that was really me?

LAMENT FOR MY OLD LIFE

Every morning is an entrance to a city. –Regula Russelle

I hated to leave that house,
fought it tooth and nail.
We've lived here so long,
it's like part of me, I cried.
Like a favorite jacket I'll never outgrow.

In this new, alien space,
I've lain awake at night,
imagining the old house
wrapped around me once again:
the scuffed kitchen floor,
the ugly green paneling,
the odd window on the stairs
that showed me the world aslant.
I've imagined my life warm and whole again,
and everyone where they should be.

I woke up today, finally
ready to give that old life away.
Silly, really, since
it's already gone. Someone said
that every morning
is an entrance to a city.
I guess I've found my new city,
strange and disjointed as it is.

Here, I imagine myself saying
to the kid that sleeps in my old room,
this belongs to you now.
Looks like a good fit.

HEARTLESS

You don't want my heart?
Fine. I will climb a hill
where the sky is wide.
The sun will be setting
and the wet grass will drag at my feet.
I will crouch there
as darkness wraps me in its arms,
and watch the lights wink on below:
highways, bridges, stars,
places I'll go without you.
There will be a dog with me,
a soft one,
and she will whine, lick my ear,
and knock against my legs.
When I begin to shiver
I will lean into her, but hers
is not the warmth
I will be thinking of.

I'll throw a few stones
into the belly of the night,
shout to flush the brooding crows,
and I will stride
                    back down.

Illness: A Conversation

I asked my feet why they could not walk
and they said, We are treading water.

I asked my legs why they buckled and fell
and they said, We are growing roots.

I asked my fingers why they had loosened their grip
on the world and they said, It is too hard to hold.
　　　　We are gathering clouds instead.

Why? I asked my eyes, which kept crying and crying,
and they said, We are waiting for the very last tear.

Speak! I told my lips, but my voice was not my own.

So I asked my heart, Who am I now?
and my heart said, The you underneath the you.

And I asked my soul, Who will I be?
and my soul answered,
　　　　The one whose heart is open,
　　　　the one whose eyes are clear,
　　　　the one whose hands are full of sky.

When Death Comes

It's so far
from what
you expect:
the difference
between
a "heroic battle"
and
an actual blow
to the face.
The pain:
so blindingly
sharp
and vicious,
meant
to wound in a way
you will never forget,
change
how you breathe,
leave the hollow air
reverberating
with shock.
Even when you know
it's coming,
it arrives
out of nowhere:
so quick,
so uncalled for,
such a terrible
gulf
between before
and after.

RIDING A BIKE AT NIGHT

Which way will you go?
There are no streetlights here,
only black, thicketed trees,
rutted pavement,
and everywhere the warm,
swallowing smell of the sea.

Test the wind—
it will change.
On an island, all roads
lead in circles.

It's no good to look ahead;
the street has disappeared from view.
Ride, instead, gazing up
toward the pale pewter path
of the trees' parting.
Turn when the sky turns.

Remember to breathe.
The cool scarves of air
whipping past
are your only proof of speed.

Somewhere in the singing tires,
the muffled groan of the sea,
the rabbited patches of starlit grass:
somewhere is your destination.

You will never find it
with flashlight and map.
You must simply plunge,
whirring,
into the dark.

PRAISE SONGS & BLESSINGS

~ to celebrate, thank, or express love ~

PRAISE SONG: A poem or song celebrating someone or something.

BLESSING: A bestowal of favor or thanks upon anything that makes one glad.

Blessing on the Smell of Dog

May the dog always smell of Dog.

May his scent seep through
perfumed shampoos
like the rich tang of mud in spring.

May the grass cling to his paws,
the loam to his belly;
may his fur hold the wind's breath.

May we forgive him
his whiffs of carrion and scat
from the treasures he gathers so diligently.

As we turn from all that is false,
may we praise instead
the warm scent buried like a promise
in that deep-hearted chest:
den, comfort, Home.

New Moon 12

DEC

50 46

BLESSING ON THE CURL OF CAT

As Cat curls
in a circle of sun—
sleek and round,
snug and warm,
a hint of ear
cocked in readiness
so may I find my place
in this shifting world:
secure within myself,
certain of my worth,
equally willing to
purr
or leap.

Blessing on the Downtrodden

Should you think we are strangers,
I will prove we are not.

Should you think you know me,
I will surprise you.

Should misfortune bind your wings,
I will fly before you to find us shelter.

Should your armor crack,
I will hold the pieces steady.

Should the crowd turn against you,
I will turn against the crowd.

Should hate mask your true face,
I will look into your eyes and read your story there.

BLESSING FROM THE STARS

(after the Passamaquoddy song)

We are the stars, who sing
from a distant place.

Yes, you are alone in your orbit,
as we are.
Yes, your light burns fiercely,
as fiercely as ours.

The thin wind of loneliness
may howl around you,
suck the breath from your fire.

But look before you
and behind you.
Look above you
and below you.
See how many other hearts are burning,
burning as brightly as yours.

We are the stars.
We sing with our light
in our vast, brilliant constellations:
alone,
        together.

TEACHER

I loved my chair—next to the window,
which was there if I needed it.
I loved the odd, crabbed hush in the room
as we slumped and settled in our seats.
I loved the quiet shift that happened—
how the air brightened, expanded,
began to hum—as you slipped in,
wild hair and rumpled sweater,
scribbling numbers on the board.
I loved how I hated numbers, had always
hated them, would continue to hate them
until I saw them sprout from your hands.

I loved the silence that slowly fell
as we tried to figure out the path
you were laying down, the tangle
of truths through which we must weave
to the heart of whatever mystery
you would reveal to us that day,
like a half-moon we might never see
unless we looked up.

Silly Love Song

If you are the blazing riff,
then I am the piccolo.

If you are the Maserati,
then I am the oil change.

If you are the midnight neon flash,
I am the silver hint of dawn.

If you are the raptor's wings,
I am the elephant's eyelashes.

You are the knife, I am the spoon.
You are the sun, I am the moon.

You are this, I am that.
Just kiss me.

LAKE'S PROMISE

I am the lake. I wait for you
    with cool, blue arms and silver face.

My wavelets lap, my pebbles gleam
    where once you left your barefoot trace.

Out in the world, you grow, you change;
    you lead your busy life apart

while here, the stillness folds and sinks
    around my deep, unchanging heart.

Return to me and I will wash
    your cares from you, O restless one.

Return from hurry, clash, and noise
    to drink the air and taste the sun.

Floating free in dizzy rings
    of clouds and sky, of fir and moss,

    with mystery beneath your back,
you'll find whatever you have lost.

I FIND PEACE

I find peace in the lazy doze of Saturdays
and in the beat of a pounding run.

I find peace in the sideways glance of morning
and in the blare of a city night.

I find peace in one pair of eyes, one set of ears.
I find peace in the flashing arms of a crowd.

I find peace in the challenge ahead,
and peace in the task completed.

I find peace in the color of water:
how it invites the light,
how it flows through us and around us,
how it becomes so many different things
while remaining itself.

I find peace when I set greed aside.
I find peace when I have spoken my last word.
I find peace when I am ready to listen.